Costume Reference 7

The Edwardians

MARION SICHEL

Publishers : Plays Inc : Boston

First published 1978
© Text and illustrations 1978, Marion Sichel

First American edition published by PLAYS, INC. 1978

Library of Congress Cataloging in Publication Data

Sichel, Marion.
    Costume Reference.
        Includes bibliographies and indexes.

CONTENTS: v. 1 Roman Britain and the Middle Ages—v. 2 Tudors and
Elizabethans—v. 3 Jacobean, Stuart and Restoration—v. 4 The
Eighteenth Century—v. 5 The Regency—v. 6 The Victorians—v. 7 The
Edwardians.
1. Costume—Great Britain—History
1. Title
GT 730.S48 197 391'.00941
76—54466 0-8238-0228-0 (vol. 7)

Printed in Great Britain

Contents

Introduction

Sandwiched between the stability of Victorian Britain and the appalling destruction of the First World War the period 1900-1918 has for us a particular charm. It would be difficult to think of a period of costume history, so comparatively brief, in which such important changes were taking place. It saw the end of impractical, luxurious female costume because the role of the woman changed dramatically during those years.

Edward VII's reign (1901-1910) is interesting mainly for feminine costume. The more privileged women were able to cultivate a gracious, frivolous and impractical dress style, while men continued to wear the sombre, formal suit established by their Victorian fathers. The flounce and frill of women's dress indicate that they had not yet challenged their traditional place as an 'ornament' in a man's world.

However, after about 1910 women began to question their time-honoured role. The suffragette movement was the spearhead of a wider move by women to take a more active part in those spheres from which they had previously been excluded — business, politics, education and sport.

The catstrophe of the First World War had a profound and accelerating effect on this movement and clothing reflected the change. Functional, simple and serviceable garments began to feature more and more. As women of the middle class became workers (either directly involved in war-work, for example in munitions factories or on the land, or merely making their presence felt in business as secretaries) so their clothing, hairstyles and accessories reflected the new image.

On the left the lady is in a single-breasted bolero jacket with three-quarter sleeves and matching skirt. The gentleman is in a Chesterfield overcoat, silk top hat, striped trousers and shoes with spats. On the right is the back view of a lady in a bolero type jacket with a large collar and three-quarter length sleeves with full to the wrist undersleeves. c. 1904

Men

GENERAL SURVEY

The change in male fashions was very slow in the twentieth century, with just a few alterations in some details. In fact, the lounge jacket remained unaltered for about a century. The First World War was the greatest influence with the relaxing of social standards; together with the growing popularity for sports, the growth, at the end of the previous century of 'ready-to-wear', longer weekends and with the adoption of the Saturday half day, the strict Victorian fashions and habits came to an end, and casual clothes began to make a stronger impact on the general fashion scene.

The Boer War of 1900 also had an effect — khaki neckties became popular and handkerchiefs could be tucked up into jacket sleeves. Wrist watches instead of pocket watches were beginning to be worn at the start of the century. Edward VII also led fashion in the early 1900s by wearing lounge suits in place of frock coats, and by about 1908 the bottom button of the waistcoats was often left undone, a mode that still persists today.

Before 1914, the influence of America on lounge suits resulted in broad shoulders with deep cut armholes for greater comfort. Peg-top trousers again became fashionable, as they had been in the nineteenth century. They were made wide to the knees and then tapered. At about the same period, around 1912, trousers were sometimes made with waistbands so that they could be worn without braces. This style was particularly practical with the casual flannel trousers which had come into fashion. The tops of the trousers were pleated into the waistband to give a better fit.

The frock coat, so popular in the previous century, became out-moded, except for formal occasions, leaving the morning coat with the sloping cut-away fronts and lounge jacket to be worn on most occasions.

In 1918, at the end of the war, demobilised soldiers were each given a civilian suit which was mass produced at a reasonable price, thus stimulating the demand for ready-to-wear clothes.

Lounge suits were worn by most men, and for casual wear, tweed jackets and flannel trousers were the usual attire. The suits were usually made of a tweed, with the coat skirts fairly long and a slit up the centre back. The trousers were narrow and turn-ups at the bottom became fashionable. Trouser presses had just been invented, so trousers had a sharp crease down the front. Lounge suits were worn with shirts that had high stiff collars with bow ties. Boots could be two-toned and have cloth tops, but by about 1910 shoes were more the usual wear. As socks were then visible they became more elegant and made of less clumsy materials and of brighter colours.

Lounge suits replaced frock and morning coats, and were worn with soft-fronted coloured shirts, although the collars remained white and stiff. Bow ties, as well as ordinary long ties were worn.

Silk hats were no longer generally worn.

Morning coats were mainly worn by professional people such as doctors and politicians, although top shop assistants also wore them. For weddings and funerals morning coats were often hired.

FROCK COATS

By the Edwardian era frock coats had become almost extinct and were mainly worn only on formal occasions, except by the elderly. Usually double-breasted they sported two or three buttons on each side and button-stands (separate pieces of material sewn to the front edges with the buttons and button-holes sewn on). The lapels (on either side often with two extra buttonholes) were fairly high, or could be of the rolled variety, reaching to the waist where there was a waist seam. Lapels were usually faced with silk.

The coat had a centre vent at the back with two hip buttons at the top. Two pockets were in the back pleats. In the waist seam there was often a ticket pocket and a breast pocket which could be placed either on the inside or the outside. The straight sleeves could be slit and have buttons or

The gentleman is in a frock coat with a single-breasted waistcoat. A top hat is also worn. The girl in the centre is in a Gibson Girl style dress with a shirt, cravat and a long plain skirt and a straw boater. c. 1900

end with just a plain round cuff. These were often decorated with braid to match the edges of the lapels and coat fronts.

The frock coat was not usually worn closed and the waist-line was lower than in the late 1890s, the front and back skirts still being of equal length, fairly long. Waistcoats worn with the frock were usually of the same material, or of a lighter colour. They were mainly double-breasted and usually had lapels and, occasionally, a collar.

Grey striped or black and white checked trousers as well as those of the same material were often worn with the outfit. Silk hats were the customary wear with frock coats.

MORNING COATS

In the early part of the twentieth century morning coats were worn either with matching single-breasted waistcoats and trousers, or with striped and checked trousers and a different coloured waistcoat. If the whole ensemble was in the same material it was often of a check tweed. Morning coats were nearly always single-breasted with three to four buttons and high lapels at the turn of the century, after which the lapels became lower in cut and were of the roll type. There was often a V-notch between the collar and lapels, and on the left-hand lapel there could be a buttonhole for flowers. The fronts of the coats were cut to slope away from waist level with the tails ending at the knees. There were back vents with pleats that ended with hip buttons. It was possible to have pockets in the pleats as well as breast pockets and a ticket pocket on the inside, besides an occasional outside pocket.

About 1906 two-buttoned fastenings, as well as a one-button version, became the mode, the most frequent being just a single button. The fronts and cuffs on morning suits were frequently faced with either flat braid or silk. The sleeve cuffs could be slit ending with two buttons.

LOUNGE COATS

By about 1902 the everyday lounge suit in the summer was usually of a grey flannel or narrow striped material. The jackets were slightly longer than of the previous period and usually had a centre seam at the back. (Previous versions had the back cut in one piece.) The double-breasted style of jacket usually had short pointed lapels with the neck opening high. Single-breasted versions were fastened with three to four buttons, whilst the double-breasted kind usually had six. Sleeves were straight with slit cuffs and ended with buttons.

Cut-away morning suit and silk top hat c. 1907

10

The lady is in a fitted coat worn over a longer frock and carries a large fur muff. In the centre is a naval lieutenant in uniform. The gentleman on the right is in a lounge suit with trousers with a centre crease and turned-up bottoms. A bowler hat was popular. c. 1914

Single-breasted lounge jackets were occasionally curved slightly in the front. The pockets placed at hip level were often with flaps and with a ticket pocket just above the pocket on the right-hand side. Breast pockets were always on the left side.

After the first decade of the century a lower rolling collar became fashionable with narrower lapels and wide shoulders. About 1912 the flaps on hip pockets could be replaced with welts and the outer breast pockets became less fashionable. The waist was slightly lower than the natural line and single-breasted jackets had fewer buttons than previously, just one or two, whilst double-breasted ones had two on each side. Some single-breasted jackets still had wide, pointed lapels similar to those of the double-breasted jackets worn earlier. Patch pockets were sometimes seen on flannel jackets.

By 1915 jackets were slightly shorter, usually without the centre vent at the back or even a back seam. Breast pockets as well as ticket pockets again became fashionable. Single-breasted styles were more popular and the collars, mostly of the step variety, were usually at right angles to the lapels. The usual mode was anything from two to four buttons. As there was no back vent or centre seam, shaping was achieved by darts from the top of the side pockets to the breast. Button-holes to hold flowers were usually on the left lapel for single-breasted jackets, whilst the double-breasted often had one on each side. Lapels varied both in angle and size.

Pocket flaps to most hip pockets were gradually replaced with a piped edge, (or a jetted finish). As the century progressed waistcoats and trousers were gradually matched to the jackets.

Suit with single-breasted waistcoat with turn-down collar c. 1905

WAISTCOATS

At the start of the 1900s waistcoats were quite distinct in both cut and design, being light coloured in summer and of patterned materials or knitted designs in the winter. As time progressed waistcoats were made increasingly of material to match the rest of the suit. When worn with frock or morning coats and striped trousers they were usually double-breasted, although single-breasted styles were worn with morning coats and lounge suits.

Single-breasted styles were high cut with a V-opening. If a collar was present, it was usually of the step variety with lapels, or the collar could be of the long roll kind. If waistcoats were cut really high to the neck a small turn-down collar

Flannel single-breasted suit c. 1902

Peg top trousers

was usual. At the beginning of the century waistcoats generally had only three pockets, one at the top on the left side and the other two at the bottom, one each side. The usual number of buttons was five, although there could also be more or less. Occasionally there was an extra vertical buttonhole to accommodate a watch chain. From about 1908 the last button was usually left undone, as is the case to this day.

The fronts of the single-breasted waistcoats were square cut with short points meeting in a wide V-shape, whereas when the fronts became sloped, points became longer thus making the angle of the gap more acute. The neck also gradually became lower cut, and waistcoats without collars became popular.

Double-breasted waistcoat styles usually had collars and lapels, although rolling lapels were also worn usually fairly high cut. There were three to four pockets, similar to single-breasted styles. There were also four to five pairs of buttons with fronts overlapping. The waistcoats generally were fairly straight across the bottom with a blunt central point. The fronts of all waistcoats were in a contrasting or similar colour and material to the suits, and lined, whilst the backs were usually just lining material, as this was cheaper. For the winter the backs could be of flannel and lined. To enable the waistcoats to be of a better fit they were fastened behind with a strap and buckle, the buckle being oblong and of metal.

LEGWEAR

Trouser legs were inclined to be narrow and could have a crease down the front (this crease was essential for 'smart' wear). Lounge-suit trousers occasionally had turn-ups and turned-up trousers tended to be slightly shorter than those without. If turn-ups were present the trousers reached to the top of the shoes, whilst the others just covered them. Trousers worn with morning coats were usually of a striped material and slightly wider at the base than trousers worn with other jackets.

About 1912 *peg-top trousers* became popular again, and these were wider at the top and tapered from the knees down. Trouser waistbands became fashionable with the tops of the trousers pleated into them.

By about 1915 trousers in general tended to be wider, and the popularity of turn-ups declined.

Knickerbockers were a kind of loose knee breeches fastened with a band, buckled or buttoned beneath the knee, and worn

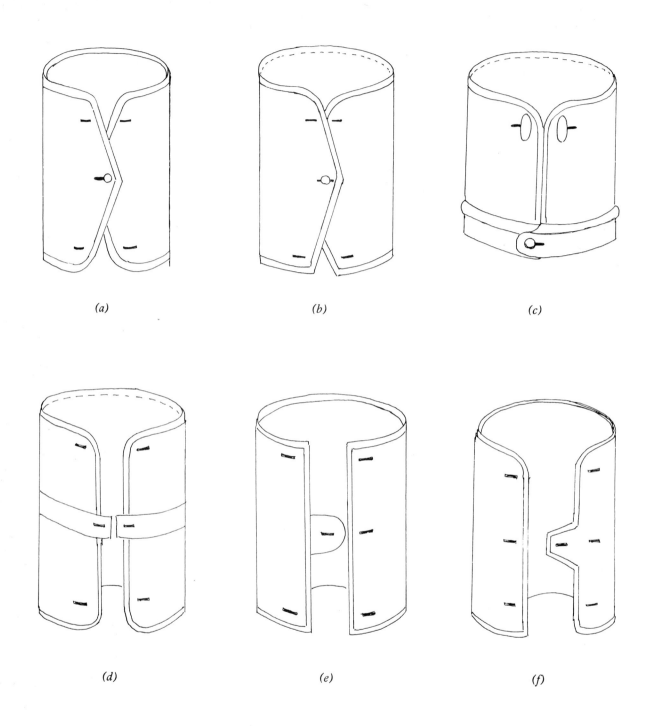

Various types of cuffs of the period c. 1902 a.The Grosvenor, in linen
b. The Stanley c. The American d. The Royal, in linen e. The Times
f. The Westminster

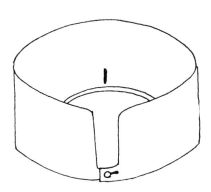

Army & Navy

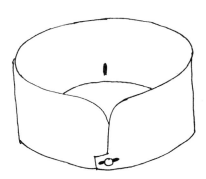

The Whitehall

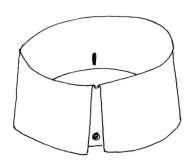

The Court

with woollen stockings. They were very popular for sports such as golf, shooting and cycling. Just before the 1914 war they became wider just above the knees, where they were gathered on to the knee band, and were later known as *plus fours*.

DANDIES

Dandies, to make themselves smarter, made the most of waist-coats which were usually double breasted. It was important for them to wear the correct attire at the appropriate times. Tail coats were essential when dining with ladies present, whilst at an all-male gathering such as at clubs or grill rooms, dinner jackets were worn. Full evening dress was worn at the theatre, although a dinner jacket was permitted in the 'dress circle'.

Waistcoats were an important part of a dandy's dress, and although not so ornamentally patterned as in the previous period, they were made in checked or birds-eye spotted materials.

The Albert top frock and Albert driving capes were named after Edward VII, whose real name was Albert.

Shiny silk hats were an important part of the dandy's clothing as well. There was not much change from the previous period in male costume, although stiff, detachable collars became higher and were worn with lounge suits as well as with Norfolk jackets. Ladies also wore them for masculine type sports such as golf. The middle and lower classes wore stiff collars made of celluloid as well as detachable cuffs and 'dickeys' (shirt fronts with false buttonholes and studs).

Lounge suits became very popular and were worn with narrow trousers which began to have turn-ups. With the aid of trouser presses which had been invented in the 1890s, the trousers had a sharp crease down the front, although the old-fashioned still wore their trousers with the creases at the sides.

Homburg or trilby (a softer version) hats were usually worn with lounge suits. Felt or wool spats were still popular from the previous period and were general wear, although button boots with cloth tops, giving the appearance of spats were also worn. They were mainly worn with brown or black patent shoes. About 1910 these were replaced by shoes which showed more sock. These then gradually ceased to be of dull colours and heavy materials, becoming brighter and of thinner wools and cottons.

Tall, white 8cm high linen *collars* were worn at the beginning of the century. Waterproof celluloid, easily sponge cleaned, was also used for shirt collars, although mainly by the poorer classes, as these collars were more economical. Collars were separate from shirts and were fastened on with collar studs. Gradually the height of these stiff collars decreased. There were several styles of collars such as the stand-fall collar, known as a double collar, and the winged collar which was a single-stand collar with the front points turned down. This latter style was worn mainly with evening dress. By about 1912 collars decreased in height to an average of 4-6cm and remained so for a while.

Neckties were of various kinds, one of the most popular varieties being bow ties. These were usually medium sized with squared ends and worn with most types of collar. For evening wear they were mainly white and worn with wing collars and tail or dress coats. With dinner jackets, bows could be either black or white, but by the time of the First World War in 1914, black ties were more popular with evening attire.

Four-in-hand ties were very popular. They were fairly long, tied in a slip knot and could have square or pointed ends and this eventually became the accepted style. Another similar

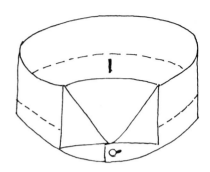

The Admiral

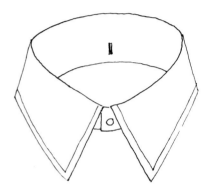

The Shakespere

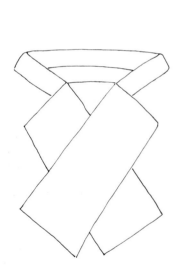

The Bond Street scarf tie c. 1902

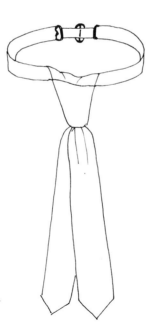

The 'New Knot' ready made tie c. 1902

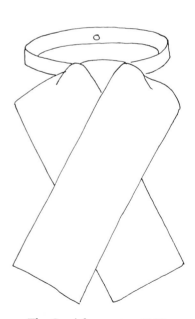

The Garrick cravat c. 1902

16

Casual fancy bow tie c. 1915/16

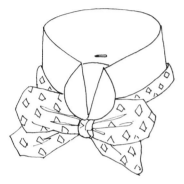

Coloured silk bow tie c. 1915/16

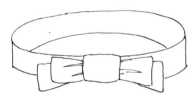

Black silk evening bow tie c. 1902

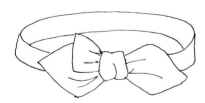

Silk bow tie c. 1902

style, the Ascot, wider than a four-in-hand, was tied or twisted in the front with the ends overlapping at an angle, and held in place with a tie-pin. A scarf could also be worn in this fashion. This style, in later years, was worn mainly with morning coats on formal occasions.

The *Derby*, with square ends, and *Lombard*, with the ends pointed, were two more terms for ties tied in a reef knot with the ends hanging down, but this fashion declined after 1918.

Ties could be in plain colours or else printed and woven in designs or spots. Diagonal stripes were introduced towards the end of the nineteenth century and increased in popularity in school, club and regimental colours. These ties were worn mainly for leisure and sports wear.

Made-up ties, that is with the knot already made and the tie fastened at the back with buckle or fastener, were available although not so very popular.

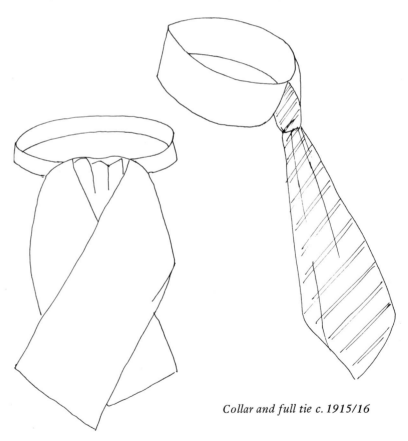

Collar and full tie c. 1915/16

The Westminster cravat c. 1902

Overcoats were made in a variety of styles, the *Chesterfield* or *Chester*, as it was also called, being one of the most popular. This was made in various forms either single- or sometimes double-breasted.

At the start of the century coats were slightly waisted with a vent at the back, and the front often closed with a fly (if single-breasted), reaching to calf length. Another variation was a sac-like coat reaching the knees. The collars were generally velvet faced, whilst the lapels were silk lined. There were a number of outside pockets, two at hip level with sometimes a ticket pocket just above on the right, and also a breast pocket.

Long lightweight rainproof coat c. 1900

Single-breasted light overcoat c. 1913

At the start of the 1900s, for a brief while, top frock coats, similar to frock coats, but longer, could be worn without a jacket beneath. These were usually double-breasted.

By about 1909 the loose single-breasted sac style was worn and by around 1915 the coats again became more waisted with a vent and centre seam at the back. Fly fronts became more general and the hip pockets were often flapped with the ticket and breast pockets welted.

Ulsters which were warmer and looser than ordinary overcoats were worn mainly when travelling. They were generally belted or had just a half belt, and could have a cape or hood attached.

A shorter, single-breasted, fly-fronted coat, just a little longer than a lounge jacket, and known as a *Covert* coat, was worn for more informal occasions. This usually had side vents and could have raglan sleeves.

There were also *Raglan* coats which were long and loose and made of a waterproof material so that they were very practical in wet weather. They were usually fly fronted and had vertical pockets and slits at the sides so that it was possible to reach the trouser pockets.

For rainwear, *mackintoshes* or raincoats were made in rubber or other waterproofed materials. The war created a new type of coat, the *trench coat*, which had a belt, and double-yoked shoulders for added safeguard against rain. These coats were originally worn by officers, but were found to be so practical that they soon found their way into civilian use. *Capes* and caped coats were still worn, the coats having split capes or wings which covered the arms, sometimes taking the place of sleeves.

FORMAL WEAR

Frock coats and tail coats for evening wear were the correct attire for all formal occasions. This remained so until the First World War.

Evening wear consisted of tailcoats, matching trousers, mainly black, and white waistcoats. Dinner jackets, similar in style and cut to lounge jackets, known as *tuxedos* in America and *Monte Carlos* in Europe, were also becoming fashionable for evening wear towards 1910. *Dinner jackets* were also known as dress jackets and were cut like single-breasted lounge suit jackets, but worn unbuttoned. Sometimes a link button was used instead of the conventional button and buttonhole, and was worn fastened. At the beginning of the century the

Waterproof cape and coat c. 1901

The lady is wearing a reception gown in the S-bend style which had three-quarter length sleeves ending in falling lace with a net or lace bolero edged with ribbon. The gentleman is wearing a dinner jacket or tuxedo c. 1901

collar was stepped and the lapels were faced with silk; fronts were square cut. If the fronts were rounded, the collar could be of the roll variety. There were generally two hip pockets on the outside which could have flaps or be welted. Occasionally the sleeves ended in cuffs.

Although tailcoats were still extensively worn, dinner jackets, first worn in the 1880s, could be worn for evening wear informally. By about 1909 low continuous collars, roll or step with wide, pointed lapels were popular and the sleeve cuffs with buttons could be slit. Sometimes a long vent at the centre back was also permissable. Gradually the long jackets became shorter, and by the 1920s just covered the seat of the trousers.

Waistcoats worn with dinner jackets were similar in style to those worn with tail coats, and if in black, were made in the same material as the jackets, whilst white ones were more usually of a piqué material.

Dress coats which were always worn done up were generally double-breasted with cut-away fronts, and the skirts hung in two tails at the back with a centre vent to the waistline.

From the start of the 1900s the dress-coat tails reached the knees and fronts were square cut to the waist with two to three buttons either side.

Around 1905 the cut of dress coats altered, so that there was a seam at the waist in the skirt parts only, although later the seam did continue to the fronts as well. By about 1912 the fronts were made to slope further back and down to the tails. A step collar with rolled lapels was faced in silk, and sometimes the collar and lapels were in one without a step. The sleeves were normally quite plain, or could have slit cuffs with two or three buttons.

Waistcoats worn with tail coats were usually white, although black could also be worn. They could be either single or double-breasted and were cut straight. By about 1912 the fronts were so cut as to form short points. The collars, if present, were generally of the roll variety with continuous lapels. For evening wear, waistcoats often had only two pockets, one either side. Single-breasted styles had three to four buttons, whilst the double-breasted ones could have four to six. Some double-breasted waistcoats with longer points often had only three buttons placed in an inverted triangle design. The opening in the front was more popularly a deep V-shape, although U-shaped openings were also fashionable.

Trousers worn with evening wear were of material to match

Folding opera hat 'Gibus' c. 1902

Hard felt topper c. 1907

the coats, and in the same styles as trousers worn in the daytime with the exception that they never had turn-ups and the outside seams usually had one or two rows of braid sewn on.

At the beginning of the 1900s a frock coat and a lighter coloured waistcoat was the correct attire worn at weddings until about 1914 when lounge suits or service uniforms replaced the frock and morning coats.

For funerals, frock coats, black trousers and waistcoats, black ties and gloves and a black band around the silk hat was the usual mode, and whilst in mourning in private whether for Queen Victoria, the South African War, Edward VII or the fallen of the First World War, black ties and black crape armbands were fashionable. Another habit, although not so popular, was the wearing of a black diamond-shaped patch instead of the armband on sleeves.

For Court wear black velvet single-breasted frock coats with the fronts sloping back were worn with matching velvet breeches or trousers. The waistcoats could be either black or white, but the stockings were invariably white with black shoes being worn. The bow ties or ruffles and gloves were also in white. During the years of the war, the fashion was relaxed to allow the wearing of black cloth breeches or trousers, and evening dress coats.

For dancing, dress suits and white cotton gloves were the mode.

Smoking or dressing jacket with silk quilted collar and cuffs c. 1913

INFORMAL AND SPORTS WEAR

The sports clothes of the late 1800s, with the substitution of trousers for knickerbockers, became formal wear in the 1900s, so for country wear tweed jackets with matching knicker-bockers and a rounded hat similar to a bowler or a soft felt hat was worn in place of the high top hats which had become town wear. *Reefer jackets*, which were always square cut, and usually without a seam at the centre back, were often double-breasted, and with about eight buttons. Occasionally when single-breasted, there were only four buttons required. Reefer jackets were always worn closed, but were less popular than in the nineteenth century, and the style tended to blend in with the double-breasted lounge jackets.

Sports jackets became very popular and were worn with flannel trousers, although they could also be worn with matching trousers or knickerbockers.

Tweed *Norfolk jackets* with box pleats, both in the front

The man on the left is in a long double-breasted reefer jacket suit with a straw panama-type hat. The boy in the blazer is in a school outfit with long trousers. The lady is wearing a close fitting dress with a fashionable fur stole and muff. c. 1913

and back, were also popular. These were either belted or had a sewn-in waistband. The top could be yoked and the pockets were of the patch type and could have pleated sides and base, so that when filled gave a box-like appearance. The collar could be of the high stand-fall variety known as a Prussian collar.

Another popular sports jacket, known as a *riding lounge*, was single-breasted with a high neck fastening and four buttons. The skirts were slightly flared with a vent in the centre back.

Single or double-breasted *smoking jackets* were worn informally at home. They were cut on similar lines to lounge or dinner jackets. The lapels were usually of the rolled style with the collar in one. Both lapels and cuffs were usually of silk quilting or facing. Fastenings and pockets were generally trimmed with braid and frogging. A popular material for smoking jackets was velvet, although other materials were also used. Smoking jackets were worn with both day and evening trousers, and could also be worn as a smoking suit when the trousers were of the same material as the jacket. The trousers were then cut loosely, similar to pyjama trousers, and fastened at the waist with a girdle.

Knitted *jumpers* and *jerseys* were worn mainly for sports. They were generally long-sleeved and had polo or turtle-necked collars which were high and close-fitting to the neck, and turned over. These jumpers were also known as *slip-overs* or *sweaters* and were pulled on over the head without any fastenings. By about 1912 the neckline could be lower with a low collar with points. V-shaped necklines also gradually became the vogue. These were then known as *pullovers*. When worn for a sporting club, the pullovers were usually white with the club colours inserted in a band at the neck or hem.

Knitted waistcoats in fancy designs were also popular. Knitted cardigans, which were first seen in the 1890s, were short and close-fitting jackets and could be without collars or have roll collars.

Most *cardigans* were fastened by buttoning. Longer styles of cardigans could have pockets either side, just below the waist level.

For hunting, black or dark grey frock coats with cloth breeches and black, plain-topped riding boots with a silk top hat or a bowler were worn by beginners in the art of hunting, but after a minimum of two years they were permitted to wear the more familiar scarlet frock coats, white buckskin

Gentleman's hunting hat c. 1907

1   *Lady in a dress showing the small waist with a close fitting skirt and trained back. The straw hat was decorated with a feather and a bow. c.1901.*

The gentleman wears a single-breasted lounge suit with a handkerchief showing from the left breast pocket. A single-breasted waistcoat with a high neckline and deep lapels is decorated with the popular watch chain across the front from pocket to pocket. c.1904.

The young boy is dressed in a frock with a deep lace collar. Full sleeves tapered down to the waist. He is wearing a large straw sailor hat and three quarter length gaiters. c.1907.

2   *A typical London street scene of a Sunday promenade around Piccadilly, of the period.
Large hats were very popular. c.1910.*

breeches and top boots which were black with brown tops.

For shooting, tweed jackets were the mode, and could have gun pads on the shoulders to protect the coat. The jackets had large pockets to hold the game. Breeches or knickerbockers were worn with boots, stockings and short gaiters. To complete the outfit, deerstalker hats with peaks front and back as well as ear flaps that could be tied to the top of the head, or tweed caps were worn

For both cricket and tennis cream or white flannel trousers and white shirts were worn. For tennis the coat or blazer was also in flannel. White striped suits with a white shirt and tie could also be worn until about 1918, after which ties especially were no longer popular. White sweaters or pullovers became the mode, and like the cricket sweaters, the tennis-club colours were knitted in a band at the neck and base. Cricket blazers were usually plain navy blue or black and could have the club badge embroidered on the top pocket. For cricket the headwear was a cap in the club colours, whilst for tennis, boaters or panama straw hats were worn. White rubber-soled canvas shoes were also fashionable.

For football knitted woollen jerseys or cotton shirts were worn with knee length shorts, boots and stockings.

Sports or Norfolk jackets with knickerbockers and stockings were the general attire for golf until about 1910, after which sports jackets and breeches with stockings became more popular. Cloth caps with peaks which were at first fairly close fitting and later became fuller in the crown were the usual headgear.

At the seaside early morning wear consisted of a shirt, sweater or blazer and flannel trousers, whilst later in the day lounge suits or morning coats were the correct wear. Grey or white striped flannel suits were also very popular. For swimming striped or plain cotton navy blue costumes were worn; sometimes they also had half sleeves. The neckline was usually rounded and the legs fairly short. By the 1920s the sleeveless versions had deeper armholes, thus giving more freedom of movement. The yachting costume consisted of a reefer suit, or a single-breasted white suit, or otherwise a reefer jacket with white trousers. Yachting caps were white topped and had glazed peaks. White canvas shoes completed the outfit. In inclement weather oilskins were also worn.

For cycling Norfolk jackets and knickerbockers were worn early in the 1900s, until the motor car took over in popularity. Then cycling costumes were not so rigid in their design, and trousers with cycle clips were also worn.

Norfolk jacket with breeches and gaiters c. 1907

For motoring, which was fast becoming an established past-time, high-necked double-breasted reefer jackets with small turned-down collars and yachting caps as well as gloves were the mode. Leather or fur lined coats in the winter were very fashionable.

FOOTWEAR

At the start of the century men mainly wore low boots in winter, and laced shoes in the summer, usually of black or brown and made in calfskin or patent leather. More elegant shoes were often made of white buckskin. Another popular colour was light tan, also sometimes known as 'yellow'. Two-tone shoes were tan or brown and white (being the most fashionable) although dark red and white could also be worn. These were known as *co-respondent shoes*. This meant that the toe caps and 'counters' (the piece over the back) could be of contrasting colour to the remainder of the shoe. Sometimes the toe caps were decorated with punched holes.

c. 1910

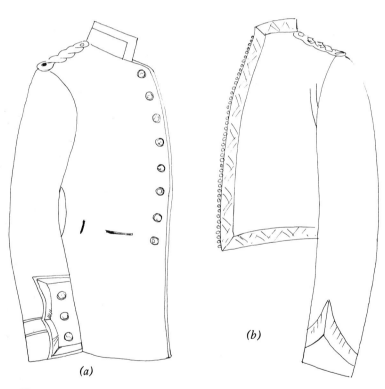

(a)

(b)

(c)

Military uniforms of the period. a. Officers tunic of the 1900/1902 period b. Mess jacket of the Dragoon Guards c. 1900 c. Guards Officers single-breasted frock coat ornamented with black braiding c. 1900

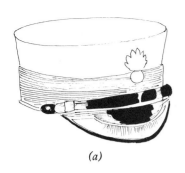

(a)

(b)

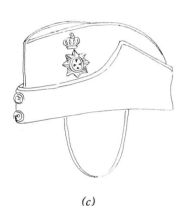

(c)

Men also wore *button boots*; these however often had a tab at the back to facilitate slipping them on. The heels were usually fairly low and made of leather. It was fashionable to have these boots lined in a striped material.

Spats of drill or felt, similar to but shorter than ladies gaiters, were fashionable throughout the era and were fastened up the sides with shank buttons and buttonholes. Popular colours were beige, light grey or white. They were held down under the footwear with elastic.

Shoes became more popular than boots; they were fashionable with rounded toes that had a bulge in the front, sometimes known as 'bulldog toes'.

Socks were made of either cotton, silk, or wool and were often clocked. They reached halfway up the calves and were held up with suspenders. When worn with knickerbockers or plus-fours, socks became more ornate and could be checked or striped, or else just the tops could be decorated. These socks were kept up with garters just below the knees, being turned down from above knee level.

HAIRSTYLES

Men's hairstyles altered very little in the early 1900s. Until about 1905 centre partings were popular, after which time side partings became more usual. Gradually the hair at the back and sides was worn closer to the head (originating with the troops in France). After about 1910 the front hair was brushed back and slightly raised.

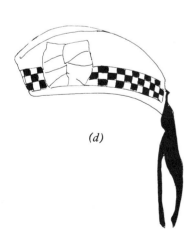

(d)

(e)

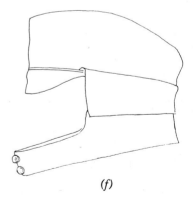

(f)

Military hat styles worn during the period a. Forage cap with embroidered peak c. 1900 b. Hussar 'pill-box' hat c. 1900 c. Field service cap with chin strap c. 1901 d. Glengarry cap c. 1901 e. Staff Officers peaked cap c. 1901 f. Field service cap unfolded c. 1901

27

Hair was kept flat with the use of hair creams and oils. Large moustaches which were sometimes waxed were fashionable until about 1920. Older men also sometimes wore small, neat beards, but by the 1920s these were quite unfashionable. By the end of World War I, both moustaches and beards as well as side whiskers and wigs were completely old-fashioned.

Silk topper c. 1907

HEADWEAR

Some kind of headwear was always worn out of doors. With frock or morning coats as well as for evening wear *silk top hats* were still worn. More generally *bowler* hats or *derbys* were worn. These were fairly flat with a brim that could be curved up at the sides. They were more usual in black, but could also be in brown or grey.

The *homburg*, brought back from Germany by Edward VII, was another popular style, made of a stiff felt with an indented crown running from back to front, and the brim turned up and bound in silk. Trilbys, similar to the homburg, were usually of a softer felt or could be made of a velour or straw for summer wear.

Lightweight bowler hat c. 1907

The *cheerer* was another style, similar to a hard felt bowler with a flat top. The *panama* made its appearance early in this period. This was a lightweight straw hat in either white or a natural colour, and was wide brimmed and worn mainly on casual occasions in the summer.

Boaters were still very popular and were flat crowned with flat brims. For evening or dinner wear, the *Gibus* or opera hat was often worn. This was a collapsible hat, the crown being supported by a spiral spring, and enclosed in the lining. When collapsed the hat was quite flat.

The Rutland homburg c. 1917

Tweed hats, *deerstalkers* and tweed caps, also known as golf caps and made in eight sections, as well as loose caps which were cut in one with the front sometimes fastened to the peak with a snap fastener, were also worn. Soft felt hats with large unbound brims were made in a variety of styles and had numerous names, the most popular being the *wide-awake*.

TOILETRIES

Men liked to smell clean and sweet, but instead of buying perfumes which were considered effeminate and mainly aimed at women, they bought sweet-smelling hair tonics or scented toilet waters.

To counteract pallor, rouge was applied to the cheeks,

Folding panama hat c. 1913

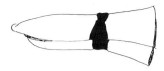

Folding panama hat rolled up c. 1913

Boater with serrated edge c. 1913

Pamama grass homburg c. 1913

whereas if the natural facial colouring was too high, another preparation or powder was used to lighten the skin.

Moustaches, when worn, were rubbed with a lotion which made them stiff and gave them a sheen. Hair was often curled or waved in the front with curling irons.

ACCESSORIES

Gloves were always worn in town, made of leather, suede or cloth, and for evening wear they were usually of a soft kid leather. For driving, they could be of cotton or silk backed with leather on the inside of the palms. Gloves were generally fastened on the back, to the wrist, with either two buttons or fasteners. With the growing popularity of outside breast pockets on jackets, it became fashionable to have a white handkerchief protruding from it.

Umbrellas were mainly carried instead of walking sticks and were tightly furled around a wooden stick or metal tube. The handles were mainly of the crook variety, although straight and crutch handles were also available.

Pocket watches were still worn in a waistcoat pocket with the Albert chain, with sometimes a seal at the opposite end, fastened across the waistcoat.

Tie-pins often had the heads ornamented with jewels or a gold design. They could fasten the ties to the shirts with either a clip or safety pin device. *Collar studs* and *cuff links*, often matching, were made in various forms. For evening wear they could be of mother-of-pearl and made to match the buttons of the evening waistcoats.

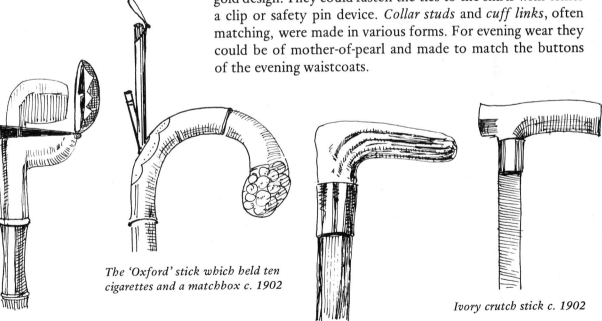

Silver handled stick used as a pipe holder c. 1902

The 'Oxford' stick which held ten cigarettes and a matchbox c. 1902

Stag horn handled stick c. 1902

Ivory crutch stick c. 1902

By 1918 most people were in uniform. Shown is a nurse's uniform, a sergeant in khaki and an officer carrying a trench coat. 1918

Women

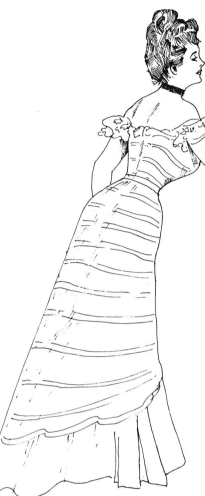

GENERAL SURVEY

A characteristic feature of the Edwardian era were the Gibson Girl styles, made popular by Charles Dana Gibson, an American illustrator. The style of clothes gave the figure an 'S' shape with a large bosom, small waist, and a large posterior. The blouses were high necked with turned-down collars and long, puffed sleeves — similar to the older gigot style. The long straight skirts were slightly flared and fairly stiff. In the final years of the nineteenth century a special corset was designed to be worn with the new S-shaped silhouette which was popular throughout the Edwardian era.

Dresses were generally in two pieces, the bodice now called a blouse and a skirt. Blouses were usually high-necked and gathered, pleated or tucked at the front. Boleros, similar to the Zouave jackets but smaller, were close-fitting coatees with the fronts curved, and they were very popular with day dresses. Blouses, by now very popular, were pouched and worn below the waistline in front. This style was fashionable until about 1905. Until around 1913 the neck ended in a high stiff net or lace collar which was kept in place with the aid of vertical pieces of whalebone, wires or celluloid. With the high, fashionable hairstyles the neckline was accentuated. Also characteristic of the 'Gibson Girl' era were the long boas or stoles which could be made of either feathers or ruffled chiffon.

The waist was usually belted to emphasise smallness. Skirts were still long at the start of the century, being gored or pleated. For evening wear when skirts were often trained, they were lifted for walking, thus revealing the ruffled petticoats

The lady is in a bolero suit with matching top and overskirt. The hat is decorated with feathers. The young girl is in a short jacket with a Peter Pan collar and gigot type sleeves. The skirt is knee length and worn with gaiter shoes. The hat decorated with ribbons and flowers. c. 1906

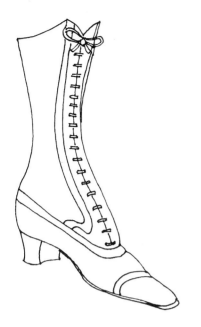

Russian-type high laced boots c. 1914

which were frequently made of taffeta which rustled with the movement.

Paul Poiret, a prominent French dress designer, pioneered less restricting clothes with higher waistlines and straight skirts. His interest in the Oriental was reflected in an extremely tight hobble skirt and tunic overdress. Kimono sleeves as well as turban headwear were also a result of his interests.

About 1915 changes in fashion became more obvious with overtunics becoming longer, whilst underskirts remained fairly narrow and ankle length.

By about 1916 plainer and more practical clothing became more apparent due partially to the Great War and also to the greater freedom of women.

In the war years many women were employed in various jobs, so fashions became more tolerant, and girls working on the land often wore either breeches or trousers. This became an accepted fashion for most workers in munitions, ship yards, etc. Another practical outfit was a single-breasted coat which just reached the knees; it had practical patch pockets and a belt. This coat was also worn with trousers.

To protect the hair from both dirt and machinery all types of mob caps were worn.

Skirts gradually just reached the calves and became fuller to allow for greater movement while high-collared coats became loose fitting and could be either long, three-quarter length or resemble short jackets. Tailored suits were often adapted to be worn as a uniform during the war and were generally in subdued colours. Women began to wear gaiters when shorter skirts came into fashion.

Soon after the start of the First World War when women joined the Services, flat-heeled shoes and boots for walking became popular. Russian-type boots first appeared in the war period. Until the end of the war, long laced boots were worn for both town and country wear.

DAY DRESSES

Dresses for day wear could be made in one or have bodice and skirt separate. Two-piece dresses very often had the blouse in a different material to the skirt, and often the skirt matched a jacket.

The two-piece *suit*, or English tailor-made, originated by Charles Worth for the Empress Eugénie of France, and produced for women generally by the French designer Doucet, became very popular. Tailored coats and skirts became classic wear for country, sports, travel and town wear. The skirts

A street scene of the Boer War period. The year — 1902 — shows the contrast between the classes in fashionable costume which was very noticeable. The fashionable lady is dressed in a profusely ornamented day dress.

were often only ankle length for more active wear, with black or brown stockings and laced Oxford shoes and long buttoned boots. The shirt blouses worn with these outfits were masculine in looks with collar and cuffs.

At the beginning of the century *Russian blouses* were worn. They had short basques and a waistband that was wider at the back than the front. Until 1906 most blouses were pouched in the front and were often lined. High-necked blouses were frequently boned for extra stiffness at the neck, but they could also have a low décolletage. Blouse collars could be squared in the front and round behind; sailor-type collars were also popular. From the beginning of the century blouses were also known as shirts. Diaphanous blouses were sometimes referred to as 'pneumonia' blouses and it was essential to wear a chemisette or something beneath. Around 1909 Peter Pan collars became modish. They were generally fairly small and turned down, and named after the character in the book of that name by Sir James Barrie.

Long *sleeves* were mainly fitted to the elbows from where they became so wide that they were gathered at the wrists until about 1906 when sleeves became wider at the shoulders in a demi-gigot style. Short sleeves could be full at the hem, and undersleeves or ruffles worn beneath were very popular. Kimono sleeves were also worn as were cape sleeves, all worn with undersleeves — a very fashionable mode. Pagoda sleeves were also very popular with white engageantes (see Glossary). Long tight sleeves which extended over the hands, ending in points, were fashionable, and for evening wear lace was very popular. Sleeves that were tight fitting could also be loose and full from the elbows to the wrist, and between about 1904-6 some were full from the shoulder to elbow, but they were always soft and flowing in contrast to the stiffer full sleeves of earlier periods.

From 1910 day dresses were normally one piece and very often bought ready-made. The drapery of the bodice top gradually became less elaborate, and the skirts plainer, although some bodices were still lined. High collars persisted until about 1912 when a V or round neckline became popular — Peter Pan or standing collars were added. Skirts varied from hobble to tunic and panelled varieties. Pannier effects were also sometimes achieved by bunching the tunics just below the hips.

About 1910 dresses with Magyar sleeves were worn quite often instead of a blouse and skirt for morning wear.

Blouses c. 1905

Blouses were generally white or the same colour as skirts and were decorated with tucks, pleats and insertions of lace or ribbons. False revers and jabots were also fashionable, and embroidery as well as false bolero fronts were also in vogue. From about 1910 blouses were usually worn tucked inside the skirts. In the second decade of the century the high, boned collars so popular previously made way for lower, rounder necklines with sometimes a flat collar. The long sleeves were usually close fitting and ended with cuffs which could be turned back, or small frills. The fronts of blouses were decorated with pleats, frill, tucks and, if yoked, embroidery on the front panels and yokes.

Around 1915 blouse sleeves could be in the gigot style with the shoulder line low on the arms, and sometimes the sleeves became close fitting to the wrists.

By about 1915 skirts became fuller, wither flared or bell shaped. The tunic overskirts could be pointed at the fronts or the sides. Skirts also became shorter and tunic skirts were replaced by flounces. Skirts which were fairly tight fitting were flared from the hips, this effect being achieved with either gores or flounces. Afternoon and evening skirts were often trained.

Ground length skirts were often longer at the back at the beginning of the century. They were either gored or flounced. By about 1904 it was fashionable to have tucks or gathers around the hips to give more fullness; another method of achieving this was pleating from the knees down. Waistlines also began to dip in the front, and the back of the skirt was held up by hooks to the bodice. There were a great variety of skirt styles in the 1900s: the *waterfall* had the tucks at the hips pleated to the waist at the back and then allowed to fall freely; the *mermaid* skirt was tight and from the knees flared out behind to give a fishtail effect. Sunray pleating was achieved by cutting the skirt on a circular pattern. Skirts were often lined to give body to the less heavy materials and some lightweight ones had weights around the hem. About 1906 corselet skirts had the boned waistband above the natural waistline and were similar to yoked skirts. Many skirts had embroidered hems and waistbands.

Overskirts, or *peplums*, cut to three points were sewn in one with the basic skirt at the waist seam, and tunic overskirts ended just below the knees. Narrower wrap-over or buttoned skirts were popular and trimmed with fur or braid. With the mode for straighter skirts, the linings were often dispensed with.

The fashionable lady on the left is in a light coat with matching fur stole and muff. In the centre is a Red Cross nurse in a riding costume. On the right the lady is wearing a bolero jacket and an Oriental influenced hobble costume with unusual feathered headwear. c. 1914

Hobble skirts appeared around 1910. They were made to narrow towards the hem, often with a bias band at the base. To prevent ladies from taking too long strides and splitting the skirts, a braid fetter was sometimes worn. Early in 1911 a *Turkish* skirt designed by Paul Poiret, and the *harem* skirt, which was a divided or trouser skirt, made just a short sensational appearance. For evening wear the harem skirt also known as a 'jupe culotte' consisted of baggy trousers gathered at the ankles and worn under a tunic or overdress with a slit at the sides.

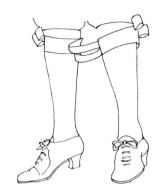

Hobble fetters or gaiters c. 1911

When women were doing war work they often wore trousers under the skirts. From as early as 1907 dresses became loose fitting with slightly raised waistlines with smaller hips and less ornate frilling, as stripes and patterned materials made their appearance.

During the First World War extravagant dress was considered unpatriotic, so simple tailored military-style costumes were fashionable. The skirts were long and worn with pouched blouses or woollen cardigans. Buttoned jackets could finish the ensemble.

Costumes were popular from the beginning of the century. They were generally worn with a blouse or shirt. The jackets could be of the bolero style, single or double-breasted. The fronts were sometimes square cut or could be pointed. Basques were also sometimes present. Collars and revers varied and were occasionally very large, but roll collars and lapels were also popular. The backs of the jackets could also be pleated. Russian style coats which were basqued and belted often had small high collars and were fastened diagonally from the left shoulder down. Around 1907 cut-away coats were also worn, the fronts sometimes being in a bolero style, and the backs longer. Sleeves were often puffed at the shoulders, being pleated into the armhole, but usually long.

By about 1912 the *costume coats* became much longer, reaching the hips or even as low as the knees. They were single- or double-breasted with long tight sleeves which could be cuffed. The collars and lapels were often in a contrasting colour and material, velvet being very fashionable. Embroidery on the fronts was quite usual.

Jackets were often closed with large decorative buttons. By 1914 the jacket again became shorter and could be in the cut-away style. Another popular variation was jackets with kimono or Magyar style sleeves, the jackets being longer for morning wear than for the afternoons. The jackets could be

Tailor-made suit with hip length jacket puffed at the shoulder sleeves. c. 1911

belted or just have half belts at the back. Norfolk and military styles with patch pockets were also worn a great deal from about 1916. Waistcoats were sometimes worn with these outfits from the beginning of the century. They were worn especially with the jackets that had the cut-away fronts. For sports costumes the skirts were usually shorter and could be of the wrap-over variety, buttoning on the side.

With *Russian-style jackets* skirts were usually narrow. From 1910 skirts were generally straight and tubular in shape, decorated at the hem with ribbons or bands of embroidery or with decorative buttons down the sides. When the skirts became really tight fitting they were often slit at the sides, up to about 30cm from the hem. Sometimes there were insets to give more width. Wrap-over skirts came in when tight-fitting ones lost popularity, about 1913. By 1914 skirts became less ornate and became shorter as the war years progressed until they were about 25cm from the ground in 1917.

Jumpers were first really popular from about 1916 and were usually made of a knitted material, silks, jersey or wool being much used. They gradually replaced shirts and blouses. The main feature of the jumper was that it had no fastenings and simply pulled on over the head. It could be fairly long to the hips, but with a belt or sash around the waist. *Jumper frocks*, again without fastenings and slipped on over the head, also became popular and could be of knitted or crocheted material.

Around 1915 skirts suddenly became shorter and flared or fluted and bell shaped; they were about 20cm from the ground.

FORMAL WEAR

Wedding dresses were mainly of white satin or silk or could be of velvet. The bodice and skirt could be in one or made separately, the skirt being trained at the back. The styles of wedding dresses usually followed the fashions of the period, and were often worn as evening gowns afterwards. Sleeves could be short and puffed or straight and long with wide lace oversleeves.

Veils, usually thrown back from the face, were of a lighter lace than previously and sometimes formed part of the train. During the First World War white wedding dresses were not always worn and a going-away dress would suffice.

Mourning dress remained black crape (worn for one year after bereavement, after which plain black dresses were worn for a further year). By about 1910 the time for mourning was reduced to eighteen months and the war further reduced this time.

Court dresses were low cut, and for young girls or debutantes white was the paramount colour with matching white gloves and feather decoration. Long trains in other colours could be pleated and attached to the gown at the shoulders or from the waist. Most court dresses followed the fashions of the day.

EVENING WEAR

Until the first decade of the 1900s evening dresses consisted of a bodice and skirt made in similar styles to day dresses, except that they were more ornate and elaborate. The bodices which had a low décolletage, either round, square or V-shaped, were lined and boned to give a better fit. The bodices were often help up just with shoulder straps which could be decorated with either jet or some other ornamentation. Sleeves could be of lace or some other diaphanous material with the bertha or fichu over the décolletage in the same material. The sleeves were full and light with flounces and puffs. A more open sleeve was a kind of hanging or handkerchief sleeve which emitted from the armhole and hung loose, sometimes trailing to the ground; the ends could be tasselled. Magyar sleeves cut in one with the bodice were also very popular. Wide sashes were popular, and they were also sometimes boned. Empire or Princess lines were much worn with satin underskirts. Tunics could also be worn over plain ones for evenings.

Blouses of the period. c. 1905

By about 1911 evening dresses were generally made in one with the bodice and skirt joined. Tunics or overdresses were still worn. The overskirts were often draped or could be in two pieces, front and back. The loose tunics had large armholes which were sometimes open to hip level and fastened with lacing or ribbon bows. Evening blouses were made similar to day blouses, but with a greater amount of embroidery and embellishment. When the décolletage was low or V-necked, drapery could be crossed over the front and the back (which was also low). The chemisettes or fill-ins were often in flesh colours from about 1915 when high collars also became the mode. Bodices could be basqued or frilled at the hem and by about 1913 when brassières were worn, they were made to help emphasise the figure, but by the end of the war a looser shape was again popular.

Flared, trained skirts were often flounced or scalloped at the hems, with the under part of the train lined with even

The unfunctional swimming costume c. 1903

Swimming costume c. 1910

more flouncing. The natural waistline gradually became higher and from about 1909 the high-waisted Empire line with an ornate and jewelled corselet and the skirts tight to the hips, became very popular.

Bodice and sleeves were very often draped. Although fairly plain in styling gowns were extravagantly embroidered and appliquéd with either jewels or beads. The delicate skirts were often weighted with lead at the hems.

Towards 1910 skirts became more constricting with the overskirt caught just below the knees with a band or ribbon. This was the beginning of the hobble skirt fashion.

Gowns made in one also became more fashionable from about 1910 with high waists, the bodice part merely resembling a wide belt or sash and held up by shoulder straps. Hobble skirts gained in favour for a brief while with the overskirts gathered just above ground level to a buckled belt or sash fastening. For theatre or dinner wear the low décolletage was often covered with a high transparent yoke and matching sleeves which sometimes only reached to the elbows. Fashionable lace mitts which were also worn were quite high and sometimes met the sleeves.

Dresses worn at dances had fuller skirts which could be sunray pleated or gored, and ended just above the ground.

Until the war skirts reached the ground, but after that they became slightly shorter. The straight or Empire line remained fashionable until about 1920. Evening dresses were of plain or embroidered brocades, satins, silks, tulle, lace and georgette, to name only several of the great variety of materials available. Wide belts and sashes which could be tied at the back in a large bow or allowed to trail to the ground were very popular.

SPORTS WEAR

Swimming costumes at the beginning of the century consisted of a short dress with trousers that were tight fitting at the knees, becoming gradually shorter over the years, and by about 1914 the legs were bare to the thighs, whilst the arms and shoulders also became visible. Around 1900 swimming or *bathing costumes* were almost always of red or navy blue serge material with white braid decoration. The knickers and basqued tunic could be in one, or separate with a knee length skirt. Other colours were gradually accepted and ornamentation could, apart from braiding, be of embroidery or bows and even decorative buttons. By about 1909 bathing costumes were sometimes made of a woven material that was more shaped to the body. Bathing stockings as well as special shoes, which could be criss-cross laced to the knees, were also worn.

Flared skirts were first worn for skating in the early 1900s and over these were worn double-breasted coats trimmed with fur at the collar and cuffs. Gloves, hats and muffs which could be of fur or fur trimmed were quite an important accessory for skating. When hobble skirts were fashionable, these, although almost impossible to skate in, were nevertheless worn.

For golfing and shooting, skirts were made a few inches off the ground and often bound with leather at the hem. Norfolk-style jackets were the usual attire. Blouses or shirts were often worn with a stiff collar and a tie, although stiff shirts and high collars became less popular. Cardigans or knitted jerseys were worn for extra warmth. When tailor-mades became fashionable, tweed suits with the jackets belted could also be worn. For headwear the hats were of stiff felt or tweed caps were also popular. Boots and shoes with gaiters finished the ensemble. Coats, if worn, were trimmed with leather to match the skirt hems, and they could be quite long.

Tennis clothes were usually white linen and consisted of dress or skirt and blouse, the skirts reaching to just above the ankles. Straw boaters were also popular. By about 1920 a tennis dress was evolved which was shorter and more functional than earlier styles. The dress was cut in the Princess style with a straight skirt and three-quarter length sleeves, but high necked. The bodice, cuffs and the front of the skirt could be embroidered. Another outfit consisted of a white blouse and white skirt. The blouse could have a turned-down collar showing from a V-necked front. A scarf or tie could be casually worn around under the collar, and instead of a hat the hair was held in place with a ribbon.

In the early 1900s habit jackets and apron skirts, open at the back, were worn over breeches for horse riding. Skirts could also be worn, but they were of the divided variety for riding male fashion. Ankle or calf-length coats were also worn over breeches.

Motoring outfits for the winter consisted of warm dress and underclothes covered by a waterproof fur-lined top coat which was long and voluminous enough to wrap around the legs. To shelter their faces from the wind soft Shetland wool veils were worn in winter whilst for summer wear they were made of a lighter gauze, and dustcoats were sufficient over summer dresses as protection. Enormous hats, profusely em-

Golfing costume c. 1907

Lady's felt riding hat c. 1907

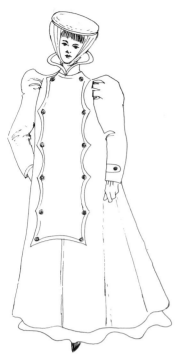

Motor coat with detachable
front piece c. 1907

Double-breasted tweed fitted
tailor-made motor coat with cape
effect c. 1907

bellished with feathers and flowers had to be tied down with veils when worn for motoring. Goggles were also an essential part of the equipment to shield the eyes. By the second decade when cars had become more advanced in design and were more closed in, less protective clothing was required, although fur and leather motor coats and veils and goggles were still necessary for the more open sports cars.

Cycling skirts were specially designed so that the backs hung straight down, so as not to interfere with the wheels. By about 1911 the skirts had an inverted pleat at the back. Knickerbockers and bloomers had become unfashionable. Blouses were worn with jackets over them.

INFORMAL WEAR

Teagowns were generally made in one and of the Princess style or in the Empire line with a high waist and loose bodice. Bolero effects were also popular and low necklines and long sleeves were usual. Pleating and lace trimmings often elaborated the teagowns. By about 1915 a pinafore style became more fashionable and was made of a light material such as crêpe de Chine. *Afternoon gowns* in the Princess line were often sleeveless with long undersleeves. The skirts were often pleated or flounced. Sashes around the waist were popular with the ends allowed to fall down the front. During the period of hobble skirts some afternoon gowns often had draped overskirts which hid the tight straight skirts beneath. Panels were also much in vogue. By about 1914 drapery tended towards one side on the hips.

House frocks worn informally were usually V-necked with or without collars, were open down the front and were generally closed with buttons.

UNDERWEAR

By about 1902, *petticoats* were no longer made of stiff rustling materials, as it became unfashionable for them to make any sound.

In the Edwardian period clinging gowns were worn over a straight-fronted *corset* which formed an S shape. The bosom was thrust forward in a type of bust improver known as a 'Neena', whilst the posterior was pushed out at the back. The waist, in contrast, was apparently reduced by the use of padding over the back, hips and chest. The corset was made with long metal stays in the front, with hook fastenings. It was worn over a chemise, the bottom of which was tucked into

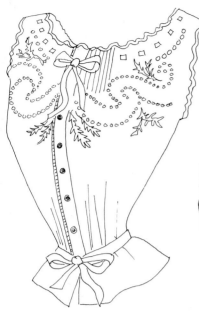

Corset cover c. 1905

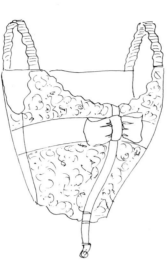

Lace brassière with elastic straps c. 1913

Girdle with satin panel and elasticated waistline c. 1915

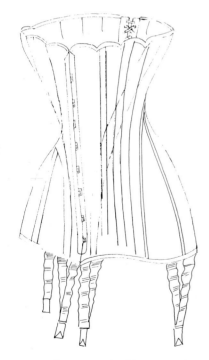

Corset long over the hips c. 1906

Brassiere stiffened with whale-bone and with adjustable straps c. 1905

Satin girdle c. 1914

44

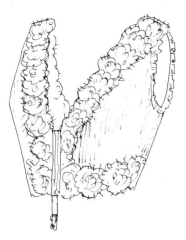

Embroidered linen or lawn
brassière c. 1914

the drawers which had become so short it resembled a sack with two short legs. The top of the chemise was pulled so tight that it supported the breasts. With the growing popularity of sports for women tight corsets became less popular, and when women began work in the First World War tight lacing became very impractical and more comfortable underwear became essential.

Corsets gradually evolved into girdles that only went from waist to groin, instead of, as previously, to mid-thigh. With this new innovation brassières were invented. At first they were worn over the chemise, but after a short while the chemise was discarded altogether. Corsets or girdles also served as suspender belts to hold up the stockings, and gradually the girdles became so small that they really only functioned as suspender belts.

Drawers of a thinner material became fashionable, mainly in black, white or pink. There were two kinds of drawers: knickers that had wide legs and reached the thighs, and a tight-fitting and shorter style, the forerunner of panties and briefs.

The introduction of *brassières* from about 1913 helped to emphasise the female shape, especially for evening dresses which had low necklines and a soft shape.

Pyjamas, instead of nightdresses, began to be worn by women during the First World War.

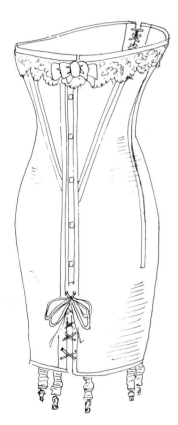

Sueded tricot corset with lace
trimming c. 1912

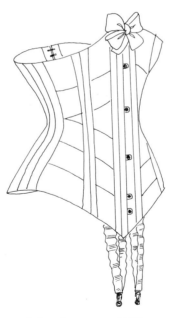

Back-laced corset c. 1905

Fancy suspenders c. 1910

Machine or hand knitted short coats were fashionable; they were also known as *sports coats*, although not worn specifically for sporting occasions. Originally they were like fitted cardigans, but by about 1912 they were made loose as well, altogether more casual and reaching the hips. The collars were flat and the lapels wide and long from the collar down to the base of the cardigan. The cardigan could be fastened with either buttons or a belt that could be tied or buckled. There were usually large pockets on either side. These short coats or cardigans were worn over blouses or summer suits and could be made in a crêpe de Chine or knitted in artificial silk, especially when wool became scarce during the war. By the end of the war whole suits were made in this style, the cardigans and skirts matching.

The general name for overcoats was the *Ulster*, which was made in many styles. They could be three quarter length or long and could be either loose fitting or fitted.

Capes and *cloaks*, full or three-quarter length were still being worn at the beginning of the century. Both cloaks and Ulster coats were often made in reversible tweed, the coats sometimes having a small cape or velvet collar attached. Military style three-quarter length coats in navy blue and a contrasting piping were made without collars, and usually had brass buttons.

Paletots were still worn and could have up to three capes attached. Basqued jackets with wide revers and high or Medici collars were also worn in the early 1900s. *Raglan* coats were also popular. A style which became popular about 1908 was cut similar to a man's frock coat, and long, the front resembling a bolero in style.

A belted coat with an embroidered edge was known as a *Russian coat*, although all types of coats had decorative bands. Long double-breasted coats were also fashionable with very large buttons from about 1910. Just after this period coats became long and close fitting. Some styles often fastened with just one button on the left and had long roll collars, whilst the double-breasted or single-breasted styles buttoned down the centre front had deep revers. They could also have a belt or sometimes just a half belt at the back.

Coats worn on special occasions were often braided on collar and cuffs and were embroidered in the front. In the summer these coats were in silk or satin, and could also be lace trimmed, or the long roll collars edged with fringing. For

Walking costume, tailor-made with hip length jacket, masculine type collar and bow. c. 1903

Walking costume with three-quarter length jacket and collar trimmed with fur. c. 1907

On the left is a clerical officer of the Women's Auxiliary Army Corps, and in the centre an officer of the Women's Royal Naval Service in uniform. On the right the lady is in a fashionable coat with a fur stole and matching fur trimming at the hem and sleeves. c. 1917/18

winter, to add extra warmth, coats could be lined. Travelling coats were often lined with fur. Fur was used for coats and capes as well as jackets, both long and short. They were usually lined in satin but could be lined in a different fur. Fur coats, when long, buttoned on the left at waist level and usually had long roll collars. Fur collars on coats made of cloth became very fashionable from about 1910.

Burberrys, named after the shop, were lightweight but warm Ulster-type coats that were elegant enough for formal occasions.

About 1914 *Raglan coats* had a fly front. By 1916 coats adopted a military style and became shorter. Some were caped and had full skirts. Collars being fairly high or turned down and deep, were often trimmed with fur. Fur trimmings were still extremely popular at the end of the war and were used on collars, cuffs, hems and even on the pockets. Some elbow-length cuffs resembled muffs. Coats made in diverse shapes could be yoked or pleated from the shoulders.

Raincoats or waterproofs could be long or three-quarter length. They were also known as Aquascutums after the shop of that name, and were single- or double-breasted. Raincoats were made of silk oilskin or other weather-proofed materials. In 1916 a type of military *trench coat*, copied from the officers in the war, became popular. It had a deep collar with revers and pockets, and a belt. The lining of the deep wide cuffs was elasticated at the wrists to keep out the wet and the cold.

For evening wear silk or velvet cloaks and wraps were worn. Styles varied immensely, being decorated with furs, embroidery, ruching, sequins, lace and all types of appliqué. They often had high collars. One popular style was a cloak, three-quarter length, gathered in at the back at the hem line. Velvet was very fashionable, silk lined with embroidery around the hem and up the edges.

By the beginning of the war coats worn in the country became more casual, looser and shorter with patch pockets, lapelled collars and cuffs.

FOOTWEAR
Women's shoes were made of various leathers. Suede was very fashionable and was made of the reverse side of almost any skin and dyed in different colours, the most popular being beige, fawn or bronze.

c. 1904

c. 1901

c. 1903

c. 1904

3   *The lady on the left is dressed in an afternoon dress with a high necked chiffon under blouse. The half sleeves and lower skirt were ornamented with lace. Three quarter length gloves were worn. The deep straw hat decorated with feathers matched the parasol and dress in colour. c.1911.*

The lady in the centre is wearing an afternoon dress in the S curve fashion. This was affected by the use of a corset which made the waist tight, and pushed the bust forward. The dress was made in broderie anglaise with renaissance style sleeves. c.1901.

On the right the lady is wearing a soft shaped two piece costume worn over a blouse. The three quarter length skirt was decorated at the hem with a fringe. Small close fitting hats were becomming popular. c.1919.

4   *The lady on the left is in a two piece costume with a basqued jacket shirred at the waist. The sleeves ended in flounced cuffs. The pocket and front were decorated with large pom-pom buttons. The straw hat was decorated with a feather. c.1915.*

The centre figures are typical of the War time period: a nurse in uniform and a man in the uniform of the latest addition to the armed Forces, the Royal Flying Corps. c.1917-1918.

c. 1909

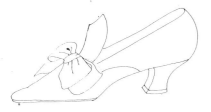

c. 1908

c. 1910

c. 1909

From about 1910 *shoes* had pointed toes with high waisted heels. They were often fastened with a bar across the top which was closed with a button. A popular colour was beige but more often shoes were made in matching colours to the dresses. Shoes which were tied with ribbons that finished with metal ends were worn a great deal, as well as shoes with stitching which decorated the vamps, toe caps and counters (the back above the heel). For fastening, buckles of marcasite or cut steel as well as paste jewellery were greatly used. Large ribbon bows were also seen.

The popular *bar shoe* could have three or more bars reaching high on the instep. With the advent of instep bars in various widths, shoes sometimes had elastic on the inside to make a better fit. With the increased use of elastic, which was now also sometimes fitted to the front of the shoe, and hidden by a decorated tab, shoes could be cut higher.

Towards 1914 buttoned bar shoes became very popular, with only the height of the heels and shape of the toes, pointed or blunt, changing over the years. High-fronted shoes were very popular, the high vamps often being concealed with either decorative buckles or decorated and punched tabs.

Court shoes (the name originated from shoes worn at Court) also became fashionable. These were plain with heels of any height. Court shoes could be high cut in the front and decorated with tabs and often had long pointed toes and Louis heels.

Open sandal-like shoes were also made with the toes closed in, but the sides left open, and the shoes were held on to the feet with a high T-bar. This style in various designs has remained popular throughout the years.

For *sports wear* laced shoes known as Oxfords or brogues were worn as short boots, the tops of which could be of a contrasting material such as a heavy cloth or even silk.

About 1917 brogues with fringed tongues became fashionable. *Pumps* were also fashionable and were made of various kinds of leather, as well as patent leather, and could have high or low heels.

By about 1912, when dancing was at its most popular, and tea dances in the afternoons were also held, elaborate *afternoon shoes* tied around the ankles with satin ribbons were made in colours to match the dresses.

For elegant occasions high-cut shoes were worn instead of boots. These usually had Cuban or Louis heels (about 5-7cm high) which were often waisted. The pointed toes were popular, as also was the long slender shape. Towards 1909 a heavier type of shoe was coming into fashion which had an upward bulge in the front — known as 'bulldog' toes. Shoes were fastened in a variety of ways: Oxford types were laced, while others were closed with buttons or bars and buttons, or even buckles.

c. 1917

For evening wear shoes were mainly in Court styles with Louis heels until about 1908 when Cuban heels came more into fashion because they were advocated for the new fashionable ballroom dances. Glacé kid, satins and brocades or soft leathers were much used, often in matching colours to the dresses. The shoes could be decorated with either beading or embroidery.

c. 1918

For outdoor wear a type of *boot* with a cloth top and buttoned to simulate spats was very popular. These boots fitted to just above the ankles. Spats could be worn especially in the winter and these were buttoned up the side.

Shorter skirts also encouraged high boots, Russian boots being very popular through the popularity of Diaghilev's Russian Ballet. Boots were laced high and could be made of cloth; some were made to look like Court shoes and gaiters. Court shoes could be buckled or have cross gartering with ankle straps. High laced boots were popularised by the Gaiety Girls. They were ornately decorated with complicated coloured stitching and inserts of various shades of leather. The toe caps could have a design punched out and the vamps could have scalloped designs. Sometimes the boots were buttoned, the buttons having shanks and the buttonholes usually stitched by hand. The vamps and quarters were often of patent leather with a softer leather or cloth for the leg part. Quite often the sides where the buttonholes were could be scalloped. Boots could also be buttoned either side of a central seam. Some boots were so high that they almost reached the knees, and were often made in a gaiter effect with material. Boots were often made in colours to match the clothes with which they were worn.

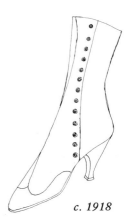

c. 1918

c. 1910

To aid the buttoning of boots and shoes, button hooks were used. These could be of any length, either long or short, and could be quite plain and functional or very ornamented. Boot buttons remained similar in construction throughout, being made with a metal loop at the back, so that the sewing on of the buttons was made easier.

With the advent of machinery, stitching on shoes became easier and intricate designs were often stitched on to shoes

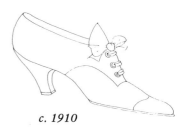

c. 1910

and boots. Different coloured threads were also sometimes used to enhance the designs.

Knee garters were fashionable and were worn just beneath the knee so that they could just be visible from beneath the shortening skirts. *Gaiters* worn by women were of wool or felt and worn over shoes, the tops were concealed beneath the skirts. They often had striped linings, similar to men's boots. They were fastened with buttons at the sides, with elastic or a strap beneath the foot.

Stockings were of a ribbed silk or lisle and in winter they could also be made of cashmere whilst for country wear were often of a heavier wool. Stockings could be decorated with clocks or lace insertions at the instep. By about 1909 the mode for brighter colours allowed stockings to be in greens and purples as well as the more sedate colours of black, brown and white. Artificial silk, first made by Courtaulds, was introduced in 1912 and used in the manufacture of stockings as well as the other materials already in use. Around 1913 pale-coloured silk became fashionable for evening wear, whilst black remained the most popular colour for day wear.

HEADWEAR

Small lace or velvet caps could be worn informally by older women who did not always follow fashionable trends. For evening wear *Juliet caps* decorated with beads or pearls were worn as well as bows of tulle. Bonnets were being replaced by hats which could be either large cartwheel types which became even bigger towards about 1910 or else toques which were brimless. At the start of the century small black hats were considered to be in good style.

From about 1901 until 1905 hats had wide curved-up brims, but for a brief while they again became small, after which the size increased even more, with hats worn at a forward angle and most of the trimmings at the back. At the start of the century, however, hats were worn straight on the head, but by about 1904 they began to be worn at an angle which could be so acute that the back was invariably decorated with a cluster of flowers or ribbons and ruching beneath the raised brim. Toques, however, were mainly worn towards the back, off the face, or straight.

About 1904 a popular hat was shaped like a tricorne. And about the same time veils that could be plain or spotted, mostly in black, became fashionable until 1908, when for a brief while they were not so popular, but they again gained favour around 1910.

c. 1901

c.1907

51

From about 1907 hats had full crowns with drooping brims and from about 1909 they became even larger. About 1908 most hats had large wide crowns which were profusely ornamented with flowers. At this period hats were worn flat on the head, and when in 1909 the brims again became larger, the crowns also became lower. This trend lasted until about 1911. As these enormous hats were unsuitable for sport, smaller hats were worn, as well as the boater and straw sailor hats which had been so popular since the 1880s.

Large hats known as 'Merry Widow' hats were popularised by Lily Elsie, who wore them embellished with feathers and flowers in the first London production of Franz Lehar's operetta of that name in 1908. By about 1910 hat diameters reached up to 180cm while skirt hems were about 120 cm.

c. 1905

For motoring, large hats were mainly worn but with a large veil, both to protect the hair from the dusty conditions of the roads as well as to help keep the hat on in the wind. Hatpins were also used to secure hats to the head.

With tailor-made and sporting clothes, felt hats in a trilby shape were worn and gradually the boater-shaped straw hats went out of fashion.

Summer hats were made of a variety of materials such as crin, lace, tulle as well as straw and leghorn. Some of the large picture hats had tulle or chiffon drapery which could fasten to the front of the dress bodice. *Watteau style* hats could be decorated with flowers above and beneath the brim, but by about 1909, hat trimming beneath the brims went out of fashion. Trimmings were always extremely profuse, consisting of flowers, lace, tulle and feathers.

In winter, hats were generally made of felt and were low crowned, usually a little plainer, decoration mainly consisting of loops and ribbon ruching as well as jewelled ornamentations. Around 1907 tall feathers or plumes at the front of hats were an important feature.

Straw sailor hats were popular around 1904 and 1905, whilst mushroom shapes were also popular from that period

In 1911 the enormous hats of the Edwardian period reached their maximum size and had to be secured to the fashionable hairstyles with long hatpins which often had ornamented heads of jewels or carved ivory in the shape of flowers and other objects and designs. As these long hatpins were placed through the hat and protruded at the other end, the sharp points were often protected with butts which were placed over the tips.

c. 1906

About 1911 tall crowned hats gained favour, whilst the very large wide-brimmed hats, (with sometimes a circumference of as much as 180cm) became less fashionable. These high hats were often trimmed with vertical ribbon loops or tall wired flower arrangements or upright plumes. Sometimes the crowns could be conical or square shaped. Some large hats had the wide brims turned up. High toques as well as tam o'shanters and berets gained favour around 1911 and 1912, and were made of beaver, velvet or straw. They could be trimmed with ribbons of satin or silk as well as tulle and feathers.

When, about 1912, hats again became smaller, the large crowns were made to fit lower on the head, and the brims also became smaller. Feather decorations which were worn either at the side or back of the hat were usually upright. When the hats became smaller they tended to tilt towards the back or side.

Around 1914 many hats did not have brims or were turned up, giving a harsher line around the forehead than previously. Towards 1914 toques became quite tall.

Throughout the First World War high-crowned toques and wide-brimmed, large-crowned hats were in fashion, similar to those worn in the Edwardian era. Another style worn was a hat with a flat low crown and a wide brim, often known as the Spanish style.

Sometimes the hats were worn tilted to one side, and trimmings consisted mainly of just a hatband which could be checked or of a patterned material and a rosette, except for elegant occasions when the trimmings were more ornate.

Women engaged in war work that required official uniforms wore a peaked cap similar to the men's in the same kind of jobs, or straw or felt hats with domed crowns and medium-sized brims. These hats usually had a hat ribbon with the appropriate badge attached. The officers of the Women's Royal Naval Service (WRNS), which was formed in 1917 wore tricorne hats with a band and badge in the front. The ratings' hats differed in that the crown was pleated with the brim all round, and just turned up slightly at the back. These hats were the forerunners of the hats worn by the Women's Armed Forces in World War Two. Towards 1915 headwear was often worn tilted to one side and sailor hats and turbans were fashionable. Veils were also worn, usually to eye level.

Until the First World War a bridal wreath of orange blossom or other flowers was the usual head attire for brides,

c. 1908

except the upper classes who sometimes wore a diamond tiara instead.

The new sport of cycling introduced a new concept of clothing, like divided skirts (derived from bloomers introduced originally by Mrs Bloomer). They were worn with small trilby hats decorated with a small feather and turned up brim. With the advent of motoring, a hat was designed which was a flat shaped cap, usually made of matching material to the coat. To prevent the hat or cap from being blown off the head when driving in the new open cars, net veils were worn. They were also useful in covering the face for protection against the wind and dust.

Around 1910 for everyday wear the huge crowns became smaller although brims still remained quite large. However, fashionable hats worn at Ascot for the races were still enormous with both very large brims and crowns.

Lace caps were still worn by elderly ladies. These were often home-made and pleated front and back to give a domed effect. Stiffened lace was arranged over the basic shape so that a long piece hung at the back to conceal the bun. The caps were often decorated with ribbon bunches and small sprays of forget-me-nots or lilac.

c. 1907

HAIRSTYLES

In the early 1900s the hairstyles of the late 1890s were still the leading influence. Hair was still dressed high in front over pads in loose puffs or the Pompadour style. The back was swept up and held in place with a profusion of hairpins and tortoiseshell combs. Back combing or French combing, as it was also sometime called, also helped to achieve the desired effect. The hair at the back was often brushed up and arranged in a plait or coil as a knot or bun at the top of the head. Another style, with the hair worn lower, was also popular. This style had the back hair with a plait or vertical coil low on the neck. Characteristically the hair was dressed in a soft fullness with thick waves. Ears were always visible, whilst the forehead was hidden by either small curls or waves. Young ladies, until they 'came out', usually wore their hair loose or plaited and tied with a large, usually black, ribbon bow.

Permanent waving was perfected in 1904 by Karl Ludwig Nessler, and known as 'Nestle', but as the whole process took up to 12 hours to complete and was very expensive, Marcel waving was still the more popular, the waves also being achieved with curling tongs and other devices.

c. 1908

c. 1909

c. 1910

c. 1910

As a full head of hair was essential for the hairstyles, toupees or 'transformations' as well as full wigs were worn by many, even younger women. The hair was dressed high and full, with the front raised in a kind of Pompadour style. Henna was a very popular red colourant.

For evening wear, hair ornamentation consisted of flowers, feathers, ornamented combs and jewelled hair clasps. About 1905 bands of false hair known as 'postiche' were worn forming a Mary Stuart hood style. They were worn around the forehead and mingled with the real hair. With the addition of more false hair, large hairstyles were achieved.

By 1908 hairstyles lay further back, but were still ample and decorated with trailing flowers, ribbons, combs and feathers. More emphasis was gradually given to the styles with the hair in large, loose twisted buns or curls held up with wide ribbon bands. The hair tended to be even wider at the sides, sometimes with a centre parting with the hair in full waves and the back hair sometimes supported by a fillet. This wideness was very fashionable, as wide-crowned hats became so popular.

In the second decade of the century wavy hair was less fashionable and although the front was softly arranged, the hair at the top of the head was fairly flat. The back however was a mass of curls held in place with wide velvet ribbons or a coil of hair. For evening wear the hairstyles were more elaborate and crowned with pearl or tulle caps decorated with silver wheat-ears and precious or paste stones. From about 1913,

c. 1910

c. 1910

although hair was still worn full, it was worn higher on the crown with soft curls at the cheeks or forehead. The hairstyles were worn closer to the head, becoming less wide, and to cover the ears the hair was drawn loosely back. The Grecian style of having the hair towards the back of the head was also popular.

Just before the First World War, in 1913, hairstyles began to alter gradually. Hair was placed not quite on top of the head, nor at the nape of the neck, but was gently puffed out with 'transformations' or false fringes or hair pieces between the nape and the crown.

For evening wear hair was worn higher on the head and this height was achieved with wired feathers which could be held in place with heavily decorated or embroidered bandeaux which were often worn like turbans. Thinner bands bedecked with jewels as well as ornamental combs and hairpins with ornamental ends were also worn. The ornamental ends could be made so that they could be bent to any shape required. Plain hairpins were, of course, also used and these were similar to the present-day ones, except that they were made of a thicker gauge wire.

During the 1914-18 War, when many women did war work, it was not practical to have long or bouffant hairstyles, so shorter hair worn closer to the head gradually gained favour. Hair was generally dressed low on the forehead and pulled back, partly covering the ears and worn in a bun or coil at the back. Women engaged in war work frequently wore a type of mob cap.

c. 1913

c. 1915

c. 1917

c. 1916

BEAUTY AIDS

Rouge and *powder* were used mainly by older women, but gradually the younger and unmarried girls also made use of artificial beauty aids in make-up which, in Edwardian times, was known as enamelling. Rouge was liberally applied over a chalky white powder on the face. The art of using make-up was still in its infancy. However actresses and music-hall artistes had already achieved skill in enchancing their appearance with theatrical make-up, or grease paints, and used face-shaping techniques with careful shading.

In the early 1900s Diaghilev's Russian Ballet which had influenced fashion, also influenced face make-up and started a mode for coloured or gilded eye shadows, which have remained popular to the present day.

With the acceptance of make-up, the preparations were professionally made of rice powder and carmine was used for the rouge. Gradually these became more reasonably priced so that most people could afford them.

ACCESSORIES

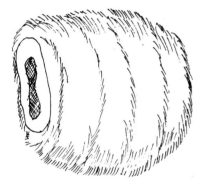

Muff c. 1904

Round *muffs* were fashionable until about 1904 when flat ones were beginning to become popular. From about 1909 large flat muffs replaced barrel-shaped ones and were narrow towards the top, generally of velvet or fur, ornamented with the heads and tails of furry animals. Muff chains or ribbons were attached so that the hands could be left free. By about 1914 large barrel-shaped muffs were again popular alongside the flat ones. Muffs were sometimes made to match fur stoles which could either be long and wide, or shaped similar to the animals from which they were made. These were usually made up of a head and several tails. Sable and fox were two very popular furs used. Feather *boas* and long *scarves* or *stoles* were also very fashionable. They could be finished at the ends with tassels or fringes. At the start of the century boas reached the ground, but by about 1909 knee length was also accepted.

Lace and chiffon were also materials used to a great extent for boas as well as for bows and cravats. Ruffles made in mainly lightweight materials were also fashionable. Feathers were adaptable to a variety of uses and were advantageously placed on hats as well as made up as hats, boas, stoles, muffs and fans.

Fans were sometimes made of feathers, especially large ostrich ones. They were popular at the start of the century, but during the war their popularity declined, being revived again later. Fans were made in a variety of different materials such as gauze or lace as well as materials with painted designs. For evening wear fans were also beaded or decorated with sequins and spangles and made to fold up.

Gloves were usually made of leather or suede and for day wear were generally worn short, although some did have gauntlets. To ensure a better fit, they were made with an opening on the inside from the wrists to about halfway up the palms of the hands and were closed with (usually four) buttons. Evening gloves, which were of a softer leather such as kid, or even of silk, were usually fastened with from 12 to 20 buttons. They were often elbow length, but the buttoning did not reach the top of the gloves, so that they could be taken off the hands and allowed to hang loosely from just above the wrists. It became fashionable around 1914 to wear the gloves wrinkled. Washable gloves also became popular towards the end of the war.

Lined or woollen gloves were popular and necessary in winter and in really cold weather over-gloves could be worn over the more elegant leather ones. These were made with a thumb piece and for the rest of the fingers a bag was constructed. These were known as *mittens*, as distinct from mitts which were fingerless gloves. *Mitts* were still worn on formal occasions and were usually of black or white lace.

Handbags were a development of the reticule of the earlier periods. Small leather bags were first popular; they could be envelope shaped with several compartments inside and an outside flap to close them. Bags became larger and were made on a metal frame which had a snap closure. To make them easier to hold they had matching leather handles so that they could be suspended from the arm. Round bags, also known as Dorothy bags, had drawstrings at the top, as a means of both fastening and carrying. These were popular for evening wear and made of brocade and beadwork. They could also be made of a metal chain, usually either gold or silver.

Shoulder purses and bags also began to appear, and these were affixed to long cords which could be carried over the shoulders or suspended from the neck.

Handkerchiefs, which in the previous century had been a popular accessory, were now mainly carried in the handbag, and lace handkershiefs were only seen with evening wear in the early 1900s.

Parasols and *umbrellas* were carried mainly for decoration.

Silk sunshade c. 1913

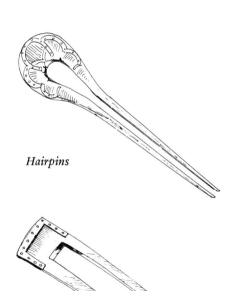

Hairpins

They were often lined with lace which also decorated the edge, whilst the main body was of chiffon or silk. About 1910 parasols were often fringed and Japanese paper sunshades also became popular. Parasol handles were usually long and delicate with decorated knobs or handles made of metal or china which could be ornamented with enamels in Art Nouveau designs. Umbrellas used for inclement weather were less ornate and were usually of black silk.

Belts were of leather of cloth, in contrast to or matching the clothes worn. They could be wide or narrow or widen into a diamond or other shape in the front. Buckles or clasps were used for securing the belts.

Hatpins varied in length in accordance with the size of hat. The larger the hats became, the longer the hatpins. The heads were of various designs which could be quite large and intricate, of metal or jewels, and they were sometimes even made of sealing wax. During the war years regimental buttons were also mounted on hatpins.

Lace during this period was an essential feature of all dresses as some form of decoration, and evening dresses were sometimes made entirely of lace. In the early part of the century white was one of the most popular colours, and in the Edwardian era the fashions were very feminine with soft fabrics, hand embroidered with lace insertions, tucks, frills and flounces.

Pearls were a favourite for jewellery and necklaces as well as brooches, rings and earrings made ample use of them. Precious stones as well as semi-precious and artificial ones were much used. Silver was a favourite metal and was used for chains and brooches which could have enamelled designs. Earrings were made to screw on the ears, so that ears did not necessarily have to be pierced. A great deal of artificial jewellery was worn and French jet, which was of black glass, often replaced real Whitby jet which again became popular after the first decade of the century. The Oriental influence was seen in the jewelled anklets from about 1916 and the snake bracelets. Rings with clusters of stones, sometimes diamonds with a coloured stone in the middle, became popular during the war. Eternity rings were also much worn during the war years.

Hooks and eyes or bars or loops made of thread were the general way of fastening garments. Press studs came into use around 1905. Buttons were sometimes fastened with loops instead of buttonholes.

Bracelet

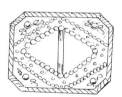

Buckle

Buckle

Neckband with pendant

Decorated neckband

60

Children

*Embroidered cashmere coat
with silk braid, laced hat and
matching deep collar c. 1902*

*Little girl in braided coat with
lace decorated hat c. 1902*

CHILDREN

Girls' fashions in the 1900s broadly resembled those of the late nineteenth century, the clothes being of pastel colours and lighter materials. Embroidery on dresses at the hems and yokes was very popular and usually, apart from a sash around the waist, the only form of adornment. Large collars attached to round necklines, and short sleeves were again fashionable.

Most schoolwear was of a navy blue serge. The girl's uniform often consisted of a dress with a sailor collar which was trimmed with white braid, as were the hem and cuffs. The sleeves were shaped with a gathering at the shoulders, full to the cuffs which could be either deep or end with just a small frill. Gym tunics or slips, first only worn for sports, as their name implies, became general school uniform from about 1912 and remained so for many years, until the 1950s.

Hair ribbons were very popular and were tied in bows on both sides of the head, with elastic under the hair at the back to stop them from slipping. Hair was often parted in the centre.

Liberty frocks, popular around 1910, were made with a low round neckline and three-quarter length loose sleeves gathered on to a cuff, under which were worn high-necked long-sleeved blouses, the sleeves also full, gathered on to a cuff.

By about 1910 brighter colours became fashionable, and instead of just serge and muslins which had been so popular in the previous decade, other materials such as wool and cotton were also used.

The younger girls' dresses were often yoked with a high

waistline, whilst older girls had the waist at the natural level. About 1914 the waistline dropped to thigh level and allowed for just a small frill or pleated material beneath the belt. This style, although uncomfortable and restricting in movement, lasted until about 1917 when high-waisted dresses again became popular.

Children wore boots until about 1908, after which shoes gained in popularity. Gaiters made of felt or leather buttoned on the outside up to or just above the knees, also became the mode for children around the same period.

Children's gaiters were usually fur lined in winter and held down with elastic passing under the arch of the foot. The gaiters completely covered the shoes and were fastened with buttons up the side. Although very similar to those worn by their elders, they reached higher up to meet the shorter skirts worn. Long stockings in either black or white were worn with shoes of similar colour, which often had a bar fastening.

Lace dress with hip low waistline c. 1905

Young girl in a party dress with a natural waistline c. 1917/18

Small girl in a kimono hand-embroidered frock c. 1913

Young girl in a pinafore dress c. 1907

Straw hats for summer wear resembled boaters and had a small brim.

For *boys* in the early 1900s velvet suits with short knee-length trousers were very popular. The collars were usually quite large, and silk shirts were also worn. This fashion remained in vogue for several years. Velvet knee breeches were also worn, often with blouses that had lace collars and cuffs. Jersey and sailor suits were also much favoured by both boys and girls.

Eton and Norfolk suits, first worn by boys in the late 1800s were still being worn by older boys. Socks and stockings were mainly in black, white or brown, and socks became longer in the second decade, reaching the knees; and were known as three-quarter length socks.

Boy in a sailor style reefer coat, sailor hat and short trousers c. 1907

Young boy in school uniform consisting of blazer and long flannel trousers c. 1907

Boy in single-breasted jacket and waistcoat with short trousers c. 1915/16

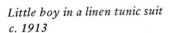

Little boy in a linen tunic suit c. 1913

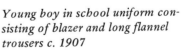

Young boy in a Norfolk jacket and knickerbocker trousers with long knee-length stockings c. 1907

Glossary

Appliqué	Decorated piece of material sewn on to a garment.
Apron Skirt	Overskirt made to look like a decorative apron.
Art Nouveau	Decorative art with exaggerated forms.
Aquascutum	Proprietory name for rainwear, named after the shop.
Bandeau	Narrow ribbon encircling the head.
Basque	Extension of a bodice or jacket below waist level, usually flared.
Boa	Long stole or scarf made usually of fur or feathers.
Bolero	Short jacket with or without sleeves, ending above waist level, round or square fronts, and seldom fastened.
Box Pleat	Parallel pleats to form a box shape.
Braces	Straps passing over the shoulders and attached to the front and back of trousers.
Brogue	Heavy shoe with punched out designs on the uppers.
Burberry	Raincoat of waterproofed material, named after shop.
Button Hooks	Appliance used for drawing buttons through buttonholes.
Button Stand	Separate strip of cloth sewn to the front edge of a coat to carry the buttons and buttonholes.
Cardigan	Close-fitting casual jacket made of a knitted material, buttoning down the front.
Chemise	Garment worn next to the skin.
Chemisette	Fill-in for a dress or blouse front.
Co-Respondent Shoes	Two tone shoes, tan or brown and white, the toe-cap and counter usually being of a different colour or material.
Corselet	Deep waistband usually boned or stiffened.
Corset	Foundation garment, boned and laced or elasticated to give a firm fit to the body.

Counter	The overlaid piece at the back of the shoe upper.
Crape	Black silk fabric worn mainly for mourning.
Crêpe de Chine	Soft silky material.
Cut-Away	Single-breasted coat with the skirts cut away in the front, the skirts at the back reaching the knees.
Décolletage	Neckline.
Dinner Jacket	Short dark coat with a silk rolled collar.
Dolman Sleeve	Sleeve cut in one with the bodice to give a deep armhole effect.
Dorothy Bag	Open topped handbag closed with a drawstring which could be carried over the wrist.
Engageantes	Sleeve ruffles.
Fly Front	Overlap of material to conceal the buttons and buttonholes
Frock Coat	Close fitting coat cut without a waist seam, with a vent at the back centre seam from the waist down.
Frogging	Ornamental braid, or braided loops for fastening.
Gaiters	Ankle and shoe covering, buttoned at the side and held down with a strap beneath the foot, similar to spats.
Garters	Elasticated bands worn high up the leg to hold up socks or stockings.
Gibus	Collapsible opera or top hat.
Gigot Sleeve	Sleeve full at the shoulder, narrowing to the wrist.
Girdle	Short light corset, usually from the waist to the thighs.
Gore	Wedge shaped material to give fulness to a skirt without bulk.
Harem Skirt	Divided skirt caught at the ankles, like full loose trousers.
Hatpin	Pointed pin about 20cm long with an ornamental top worn to secure hats to the coiffure.
Heel, Cuban	Sole ends at top of heel.
Heel, Louis	Sole continous with heel.
Hobble Skirt	Very narrow tapered to the ankles skirt, sometimes with a side slit to facilitate walking.
Homburg	Hard felt hat with indentation in the crown and rolled up brim and bound with ribbon.
Jabot	Lace type of cravat or frill down the front of a bodice or shirt.
Jersey	Stretchy knitted material, or a type of jumper.
Jet	Black mineral, brightly polished, popular for jewellery, ornaments and buttons, especially for periods of mourning.

Jetted Pockets	Pockets piped or bound with a strip of self material.
Juliet Cap	Close fitting cap made of net, decorated with beads or jewels.
Jumper	See pullover.
Jupe-Culotte	See Turkish skirt.
Kimono Sleeves	Oriental type sleeves cut in one with the garment.
Knee Breeches	Breeches fitted to the knees, similar to knickerbockers which had a fullness.
Knickerbockers	Loose type of knee breeches with a band at the knees.
Leghorn	Wheat straw from Tuscany used for hat making.
Lisle	Twisted cotton thread used for making stockings.
Lounge Suit	Short skirted jacket, slightly fitted with rounded corners, worn with matching trousers.
Magyar Sleeve	Sleeve cut in one with the bodice, but not as loose fitting as other sleeves of this type.
Mittens	Gloves with a thumb and one section for the other four fingers.
Mitts	Fingerless gloves.
Morning Coat	See frock coat.
Muff	Soft long bag, open at both ends to place the hand in for keeping warm.
Norfolk Jacket	Tweed jacket with box pleats, usually belted and with patch pockets.
Oxford Shoes	Shoes with facings sewn on to carry the laces.
Pagoda Sleeve	Long narrow sleeve widening at the wrist to reveal an under-sleeve.
Paletot	Long fitted overcoat.
Panama Hat	Hat made of plaited Toquilla leaf fibres.
Pannier	Skirt drapery bunched up at the hips.
Patent Leather	Specially treated and varnished as well as laquered leather.
Peg-Top Trousers	Trousers cut full around the hips, narrowing at the ankles.
Peplum	Overskirt hanging in points, or an extended basque to give an overskirt effect.
Peter Pan Collar	Flat collar about 8 cm wide attached to a round neckline and closed at the front, ending in rounded ends.
Piping	Narrow bias material folded and used as an edging or seam finish.
Piqué	Raised rib or honeycomb effect cotton material.
Plus Fours	Type of voluminous breeches, so called when breeches were measured to the knees plus four inches.

Polo Neck	Round closed neck of a jumper or shirt.
Pompadour Hairstyle	Hair brushed back off the face and high at the back.
Postiche	Artificial hairpiece or wig worn in addition to own hair.
Princess Line	Shaped dress cut in one without a waist seam.
Prussian Collar	High stand-fall collar, the ends almost meeting in front.
Pullover	Garment without any form of fastening, being pulled on over the head.
Quarter	Back part of upper shoe covering the heel.
Raglan Coat Sleeve	Sleeve cut in one with the shoulder so that no shoulder seam is necessary, thus making the coat more waterproof.
Reticule	Small handbag, usually of silk, brocade or beading.
Russian Blouse	Usually hip length with full sleeves and the standing collar opening at the left side. Collar and cuffs usually embroidered.
Sac	Short overcoat.
Shank Button	Button with metal loop at the back attached to sew the button on.
Slip Over	See pullover.
Spats	Short gaiters to the ankles, buttoning on outer edge, with a strap under the foot.
Sunray Pleats	Pleats radiating from one place.
Suspender Belt	Wide girdle-like belt with suspenders attached to hold up stockings.
Tablier	Decorated front panel of skirt.
Toe-Cap	Front upper part of shoe by the toes, sometimes of a different colour to the rest.
Toque	Close-fitting brimless hat.
Tricorne	Three cornered hat.
Trilby	Soft felt hat named after *Trilby* by George du Maurier.
Tucks	Folds of material stitched down.
Tunic Overskirt	Blouse or bodice falling over the skirt.
Turban	Brimless hat consisting of folds of material.
Turkish Skirt	Full skirt divided into loose trousers.
Turn-Ups	Base of trousers turned up a few centimeters.
Turtle Neck	Knitted jersey sweater with long tube-like collar without an opening, folded down.
Tuxedo	American name for dinner jacket.
Ulster	male: Belted overcoat. female: Overcoat, sometimes caped.
Vamp	Upper part of shoe which covers the front.

Vent	Vertical slit from base of hem.
Watteau Hat	Straw hat profusely embellished with feathers and ribbon — named after the French painter Jean-Antoine Watteau.
Welted Pocket	Slit pocket with a cord sewn to the open edges for added strength.
Wing Collar	Also known as Piccadilly — Stiffened standing collar with pointed turned-back tabs.
Yoke	Top part of bodice, blouse or coat, to which the lower part is sewn.
Zouave Jacket	Short jacket with rounded fronts, closed at the neck only.

Select Bibliography

Amphlett, Hilda, *Hats*, Richard Sadler 1974

Arnold, J., *Handbook of Costume*, Macmillan 1973
        Patterns of Fashion 2 Vols., Macmillan 1972

Asser, Joyce, *Historic Hairdressing*, Pitman 1966

Bennett-England, Rodney, *Dress Optional*, Peter Owen 1967

Boucher, F., *History of Costume in the West*, Thames & Hudson 1967; *20,000 Years of Fashion*, Abrams

Bradfield, N., *Costume in Detail, Women's Dress 1730-1930*, Harrap 1968
        Historical Costumes of England, Harrap 1958

Braun-Ronsdorf, M., *The Wheel of Fashion*, Thames and Hudson 1964

Brooke, Iris, *Footwear*, Pitman 1972; *History of English Costume*, Methuen 1937; *English Children's Costume*, A & C. Black 1965

Buck, Anne, *Victorian Costume & Costume Accessories*, Herbert and Jenkins 1961

Calthrop, D.C., *English Dress from Victoria to George V*, Hall and Chapman 1934

Carter, Ernestine, *Twentieth Century Fashion*, Eyre Methuen 1975

Cassin-Scott, J., *Costume & Fashion 1960-1920*, Blandford 1971

Contini, M., *The Fashion from Ancient Egypt to the Present Day*, Hamlyn 1967

Cooke, P.C., *English Costume*, Gallery Press 1968

Courtais, G. de, *Women's Headdress and Hairstyles*, Batsford 1971

Cunnington, C.W., P.E., *Costume in Pictures*, Studio Vista 1964

Cunnington, C.W., and Mansfield, A., *Handbook of English Costume in the 20th Century*, Faber & Faber 1970

Davenport, M., *The Book of Costume*, Bonanza 1968

DeAntfrasio, Charles & Roger, *History of Hair*, Bonanza 1970

Dorner, Jane, *Fashion*, Octopus 1974

Ewing, E., *History of Twentieth-Century Fashion*, Batsford 1974

Fairholt, F.W., *Costume in England*, G. Bell & Sons Ltd 1885

Françoise, Lejeune, *Histoire du Costume*, Edition Delatain

Garland, M., *The Changing Face of Beauty*, Weidenfeld & Nicolson 1957; *History of Fashion*, Orbis 1975

Gernsheim, Alison, *Fashion and Reality*, Faber and Faber 1963

Gorsline, D., *What People Wore*, Bonanza 1951

Gunn, Fenja, *The Artificial Face*, David and Charles 1973

Hansen, H., *Costume Cavalcade*, Methuen 1956

Harrison, Molly, *Hairstyles and Hairdressing*, Ward Lock 1968

Kelly, Mary, *On English Costume*, Deane 1934

Laver, James, *Concise History of Costume*, Thames & Hudson 1963; *Costume Through the Ages*, Thames & Hudson 1964 *Dandies*; Weidenfeld and Nicolson 1968; *Dress*, John Murray 1950

Lister, Margot, *Costume,* Herbert Jenkins 1967

Moore, D., *Fashion Through Fashion Plates 1771-1970*, Ward Lock 1971

Norris, Herbert, *Costume and Fashion*, J.M. Dent 1924

Pistolese & Horstig, *History of Fashions*, Wiley 1970

Saint-Laurent, C., *History of Ladies Underwear*, Michael Joseph 1968

Schofield, Angela, *Clothes in History*, Wayland 1974

Streatfield, Noel, *Shoes*, Franklin Watts 1971

Truman, N., *Historic Costuming*, Pitman 1936

Waugh, Norah, *The Cut of Men's Clothes 1600-1900*, Faber & Faber 1964 *The Cut of Women's Clothes 1600-1930*, Faber & Faber 1968

Wilcox, R.T., *Dictionary of Costume*, Batsford 1970; *The Mode in Costume*, Scribner's 1942; *The Mode in Hats and Headdress*, Scribner's 1948

Wilkerson, Marjorie, *Clothes*, Batsford 1970

Wilson, E., *History of Shoe Fashions*, Pitman 1969

Yarwood, D., *English Costume from the 2nd Century BC to the Present Day*, Batsford 1975; *Outline of English Costume*, Batsford 1967

Pictorial Encyclopedia of Fashion, Hamlyn 1968

Index